Padraic Pearse

Selected Poems: Rogha Dánta

Edited by Dermot Bolger
Introduced by Eugene McCabe
Iar-fhocal le Michael Davitt

NEW
ISLAND
BOOKS

Dublin

Padraic Pearse
Selected Poems: Rogha Dánta
is first published in 1993 by
NEW ISLAND BOOKS
2 Brookside
Dundrum Road
Dublin 14
Ireland

ISBN 1 874597 45 6 (hardback)
ISBN 1 874597 50 2 (softback)

Introduction © Eugene McCabe, 1993
Iar-fhocal © Michael Davitt, 1993
Poem © Dermot Bolger, 1986, 1993

New Island Books receives financial support from
The Arts Council (An Chomhairle Ealaíon),
Dublin, Ireland.

A catalogue record for this book is available from
The British Library.

Cover design by Jon Berkeley.
Typeset and designed by Graphic Resourses.
Printed in Ireland by Colour Books Ltd., Balboyle.

Contents

Irish Poems

Introduction

Eugene McCabe

Padraic Pearse: at the mention of his name two obvious words occur: myth and martyr.

Myth: n. GR. *mythos*, a fable, a fiction, a legend, a falsehood. Myth is neither religion nor history nor philosophy nor poetry and yet in a sense it is all of these. In most cultures, at certain periods of their history, myth can be used to justify actions that tend to be both irrational and dangerous.

Martyr: n. GR. *martur*, witness. One who sacrifices life for the sake of any principle or cause, to put to death for adhering to what one believes to be the truth. A Zealot, one obsessed with a noble imaginings of death and immortality.

As I begin to re-read his poetry, I become aware again of the kind of man he was, how he lived and especially how he died. Unavoidably this weighs our responses. Whether the poet be Wilde or Wordsworth, Larkin or Lorca. What we know of the life colours what we read, makes judgement far from easy and while definitions from a dictionary are a starting point the sum of any man adds up to a great deal more than two words.

In Pearse's case, to myth and martyr we must add: storyteller, dramatist, pageant maker, puritan, school-teacher, actor, headmaster, journalist, editor, orator and monarchist. He was also a Republican, a liberal who was quasi racist, a Gaelic, French and Classical scholar, a recluse, an indefatigable letter writer (mostly begging funds for St Enda's) a kindly and generous son, a patient and loving brother, a sincerely practising catholic, a

7

severely non practising homosexual, commandant general commanding the army of the Irish Republic and First President of Ireland. Apart from this, he was also ambitiously a poet in both Irish and English who was growing in stature when he was executed at the age of 36, and because he was at the forefront of so much thinking we tend nowadays to suspect, we have to remind ourselves what some of his contemporaries and biographers have written and said about him.

James Connolly: *"We do not think that the old heart of the earth needs to be warmed with the red wine of millions of lives. We think anyone who does is a blithering idiot."* That was 1915, a year later Connolly wrote: *"Without the shedding of blood there is no redemption."* There is no doubt that it was Pearse who persuaded Connolly to change his mind. That implies an extraordinary force of personality.

Michael Collins: *"Connolly I'd follow into hell: Pearse I'd have to think about."*

La Roux: Biographer: *"Pearse was more than a patriot. He possessed all the qualities which go to making a saint. It would not be astonishing if Pearse were to be canonised some day."*

Joe Dolan: An Ardee business man who gave generously towards St Enda's without the smallest return or the smallest complaint: *"Poor Padraic, Poor Padraic".*

McDonagh and Plunkett: Both friends and signatories of the proclamation and better poets referred to him as P.O.P. meaning: *"Poor old Pearse"* .

Mary Hayden, a female friend 17 years older: *"The lower side of women or even their lighter side, he very little understood. Anything coarse disgusted him. Never, in all the years I knew him did I ever hear from his lips even the mildest swear-words."*

Ruth Dudley Edwards, the wisest and most objective of his biographers: *"His achievements never measured up to his inflated aspirations. He failed like many others to save the living Irish language. He failed to inspire a new and glorious epoch in Gaelic literature. He failed through his arrogance to maintain a successful school. He failed to bring about a free, united and Gaelic Ireland, but he achieved triumphantly his greatest ambition of all; 'I care not though I were to live but one day and one night provided my fame and my deeds live after me'."*

General Blackadder, President of the court martial: *"I have had to condemn to death one of the finest characters I have ever come across. I don't wonder that his pupils adored him."*

Pearse on himself: *"I see my role in part as sacrifice for what my mother's people have suffered, atonement for what my father's people have done."*

Then you take down his *Collected Works* and open it on an essay called *Aspects of Irish Literature*, which he wrote when he was eighteen:

"My friend Mr McDonagh recently pointed out that the dramatic lyric link is almost as old in Irish as poetry itself. He quotes the monologue of Eve published by Dr. Kuno Meyer in Eriu as a good example of the early Irish dramatic lyric, telling in those vivid nervous lines of the Dándíreach clear and simple and thoughts of passion or emotion—poems that translate into all languages that in translation they appear almost too simple. Mr. McDonagh translates this poem almost word for word.

I am Eve, great Adam's wife,
I that wrought my Children's loss,
I that wronged Jesus of Life,
Mine by right had been the cross.

I a kingly House forsook,
Ill my choice and my disgrace,
Ill the counsel that I took
Withering me and all my race,

I that brought the winter in
And the windy glistening sky,
I that brought terror and sin,
Hell and pain and terror, I."

McDonagh is rightly praised. It's haunting. The images are startling and beautiful, but what it's implying is lousy stuff at any time in any language. Eve, the first universal woman not only ruins her husband, her children and her nation, she is also blamed for the crucifixion of Christ and earns the terror of damnation, the shame, bondage and loneliness of Mother Ireland which Pearse was to translate so effectively fourteen years later.

The essay continues:

"How much richer might European Literature have been had the story of Cuchulainn become a European possession! For the story of Cuchulainn I take to be the finest epic stuff in the world: As we have it, it is not the most finely-finished epic, but it is I repeat the finest epic stuff. The story is greater than any Greek story, the tragedy as pitiful as any Greek tragedy yet at the same time, more exultant. For the story of Cuchulainn symbolises the redemption of man by a sinless God. The curse of primal sin lies upon a people. Personal sin brings doom to their doors: a youth, free from the curse, akin with them through his mother but through his father

10

divine, redeems them by his valour; and his own death comes from it. It is like a retelling (or is it a foretelling?) of the story of Calvary."

It's all there when he was eighteen! The extravagant claims, the overwhelming conviction, the foretelling, the mystic blending of savage myth with Calvary which reappears again and again in his poetry. He catches Christ by the scruff of the neck and holds him up like an emblem, a mascot, a threat, a shield, an accusation, an invisible ally; taunting, begging, boasting, praying with a kind of rythmic rhetorical hysteria.

And now I speak, being full of vision;
I speak to my people, and I speak in my people's
    name to the masters of my people.
I say to my people that they are holy, that they are
    august, despite their chains,
That they are greater than those that hold them,
    and stronger and purer,
That they have but need of courage, and to call on
    the name of their God,
God the unforgetting, the dear God that loves the
    peoples
For whom He died naked, suffering shame.
And I say to my people's masters: Beware,
Beware of the thing that is coming, beware of the
    risen people,
Who shall take what ye would not give. Did ye think
    to conquer the people,
Or that Law is stronger than life and than men's
    desire to be free?
We will try it out with you, ye that have harried and
    held,
Ye that have bullied and bribed, tyrants, hypocrites,
    liars !

The dear God that loves his people is clearly a Gael, holy and pure and humble and has no time for the Anglo-bullies who are hypocrites and liars:

> Oh king that was born
> To set bondsmen free,
> In the coming battle,
> Help the Gael!

Then and now it's an unchristian polemic and as we read, the dictums of Christ recur..."My kingdom is not of this world"... "love your enemies"... "render unto Ceasar"... etc and a dozen other instances where it is clear that Christ is not a national leader and will not be drawn into political dispute, whereas political passion and dispute is what Pearse is all about. This makes it well nigh impossible to separate the poetry from this vision of himself as a latter day blend of Christ and the noble warrior Gael. He has one theme, one passionate brooding intention; to work and teach, to write and fight, and above all to die in an exemplary manner for the motherland and very specifically for his mother's land, her language, her culture and her freedom.

> One man can free a people
> As one man redeemed the world,
> I will take no pike,
> I will go into battle with bare hands,
> I will stand up before the Gall
> As Christ hung naked before men on
>   a tree.

It's bloody crazy, bloody embarrassing but so profoundly deathly serious and heroic that only the most cynical and hostile can fail to be affected. Not only did he want to die, he wanted to die, and sacrificially, for a variety of reasons: to be absolved for the failure of his two schools, St Ita's and St Enda's, to be a soldierly saviour and noble exemplar, to escape the aftermath of rebellion and war, the bandaging and unbandaging of the terrible wounds of civil strife, the bitterness that sours political settlements, the jostling and grafting, "the greasy hand in the till", the aping of international nothingness far removed from his dream of revitalising the heroic past, and possibly most importantly of all, to end the private sexual torment that comes up from the page with an anguished reality. Poem after poem deals with sin and desire, repression and suffering and the very real dread and longing for "That Undiscovered Country" which lies ahead. There are six verses in the threnody "Renunciation". The first lines of each quatrain and the final quatrain are very telling.

> Naked I saw thee...
> I heard thy music...
> I tasted thy mouth...
> I blinded my eyes...
> I turned my back...
>
> I have turned my face
> To this road before me,
> To the deed that I see
> And the death I shall die.

And again:

I have squandered the splendid years that the Lord
    God gave to my youth
In attempting impossible things, deeming them
    alone worth the toil.
Was it folly or grace? Not men shall judge me, but
    God.

And yet again:

> Long to me thy coming,
> Old henchman of God,

O friend of all friends,
To free me from my pain.

As a poet he is not boring, not bad and from time to time he wrote lines and lyrics that none of us here can ever forget, but we know that to outsiders they read like an outpouring of a megalomaniac with a death wish. Certainly rereading him twenty-five years on, there is a marked lack of humour; a kind of po-faced solemnity about the glory of the Gaelic past, the tendency to blame all Ireland's ills on the jackboot and vulgarity of his father's Island (his father was English), and this he combines with a zealous racism not far removed from Nazism.

Patrick Kavanagh all his life tended to be repetitive about the importance of humour in prose and verse. He was right. A poet like Wordsworth is now perceived as a dreary nineteenth century green who wrote stunningly beautiful verse about life and nature, though most people who met and heard of him once (apart from besotted admirers) went miles out of their way to avoid having to listen to him again. There is something of this obsessional drive in the personality of Pearse which transmits to his verse. He was aware of it. In an open letter to himself in *An Barr Buadh*, he says: *"Pearse you are too dark in yourself. You don't make friends with the Gaels. You avoid their company. Is it your English blood that is the cause of that I wonder."*

Partly perhaps. His humour (or a lack of it) was that of a strict headmaster ringed by a captive audience of admiring schoolboys. In the real world his "passionate intensity" was inclined to wear others down. On the eve of his greatest triumph (the vivid rhetorical poetry of the O'Donovan Rossa oration) he was on a train with his brother Willie returning from the West. Desmond Ryan's description is very graphic:

"In the carriage half way to Dublin a truculent and drunken countryman launched into the carriage blowing foul smoke-clouds over all the ladies and flourishing a bottle of whisky with an invitation to us all to take a swig. Pearse came down from heaven where he weaved the phrases of his oration with an imperious order to the countryman to behave himself and stop smoking in a non-smoking carriage under pain of instant removal. The countryman issued a general invitation to all of us to light up and not mind the pig, and until he left the carriage many stations onward, he kept up a chorus of: 'Don't mind the pig, enjoy yourselves!' Sometimes he turned to Pearse and addressed him by name as: 'You pig, pig, pig!' Pearse sat in fist-clenched silence, his face flushed while Willie laughed quietly, warning his brother with looks to say no more to the infuriated combination of clay pipe, wild hat and whisky bottle at his elbow. We reached Dublin on the very eve of the Rossa funeral and found it electrified with the preparations for the lying in state and the march to Glasnevin. All the peace of the hills and lakes fell from us suddenly."

Pearse's first reaction to coarseness (to reality) is to intervene with headmasterly stiffness, not unlike his initial reaction to Synge's *Playboy* in a review which he later revised and regretted:

"Mr Synge is using the stage with bitter contempt for all that is fine and worthy not merely in Christian morality but in human nature itself. He has produced a brutal glorification of violence."

In the light of what we now know that last sentence must be one of the most inadvertant ironies ever written. The *Playboy* as we know is full of life and light of subtlety and laughter and like all great plays it's a morality play in disguise. It has done nothing this past eighty years but provoke, gladden and entertain. Synge regarded God the father as a black comedian with a son markedly lacking in humour and the holy ghost and holy Catholic Church as a supernaturally hilarious pair: a healthy and harmless irreverence. Pearse's mystic blather ended in a welter of blood and a "glorification of violence" which still continues. The drunk on the train is closer to the real Ireland and as deserving of poetry as *Mise Éire* wrapped in her bloody flag and plotting vengence with her mad son.

Most of us would identify more with Willie's laughing reaction than his brother's severe reprimand. It's this unsmiling trait that left Pearse so wide open for rude comment about poem and story titles which he refused to change, such as " Poll an Phiobaire" "The Piper's Hole", "Brigid na Gaoihe" "Brigid of the Wind", and more especially "A Mhic na gCleas", a blameless and charming lyric about childhood innocence and adult-guilt. Pearse translated it to "Little lad of the Tricks". Both McDonagh and Plunkett warned him that it would be, could be, misinterpreted. Pearse was unbending and refused to bow to coarseness:

> Raise your comely head
> Till I kiss your mouth:
> If either of us is the better of that
> I am the better of it.
>
> There is a fragrance in your kiss
> That I have not found yet
> In the kisses of women
> Or in the honey of their bodies.
>
> Lad of the grey eyes,
> That flush in thy cheek
> Would be white with dread of me
> Could you read my secrets.

He who has my secrets
Is not fit to touch you:
Is not that a pitiful thing,
Little lad of the tricks?

Oscar Wilde's death in 1900 must have been world news when Pearse was twenty. They were born a few streets apart. I can find no written or spoken reference to Wilde in the biographies or "Collected Letters". Their lives could not have been more different nor their deaths, the expatriate from Merrion Square saying it was the wallpaper in a Paris bedroom that was killing him, the patriot from Brunswick Street writing from Kilmainham prison on the morning of his execution to his mother and ending the letter "I will call to you in my heart at the last moment". No matter how we resist or rationalise or mutter reservations it's imperishable stuff... The predawn light, the steel staircase, the stonebreakers yard, the scuff of leather on gravel, the marching and military shouting, the granite wall, the firing squad, Willie Pearse desolate: "We heard only the volley that took him", and that last poem, "The Wayfarer", which he wrote while under court-martial. Lines from it have remained with me all my life:

Or little rabbits in a field at evening,
Lit by a slanting sun,
Or some green hill where shadows drifted by
Some quiet hill where mountainy man hath sown
And soon would reap; near to the gate of Heaven;
Or children with bare feet upon the sands
Of some ebbed sea, or playing on the streets
Of little towns in Connacht,
Things young and happy.

It may be sampler poetry but because of the context it is overwhelming.

It must have been close to the Easter break in 1952. I was one of a group in the student's canteen at University College Cork, both genders, different faculties. During a silence round the table Sean O Riada began to quote quietly and naturally as though to himself:

Mise Éire:
Sine mé ná an Chailleach Bhéarra.

Mór mo ghlóir:
Mé a rug Cú Chulainn cróga.

Mór mo náir:
Mo chlann féin a dhíol a máthair.

Mise Éire:
Uaigní mé ná an Chailleach Bhéarra.

The effect I remember was very moving. Years later O Riada wrote that haunting melancholy music to match the words. Is there a word to describe that kind of emotion? Nationalism? Tribalism? Atavism (the father of a great grandfather, from Avus a grandfather, resemblance to a remote ancestor, a reversion to the primitive, an obscure sense of belonging), whatever it means it's something we should now be wary of; it can make wise men think and do very unwise things.

Before the Rising Yeats wrote: "Pearse is a dangerous man, he has the vertigo of self sacrifice". Deeply affected by the rising Yeats then wrote: "A terrible beauty is born". That beauty has long since grown savage and bitter, ugly and blind.

We have a lovely old garden here full of myth and things long withered. It is time to bury the dead things, dig it over and plant again.

English Poems

THE FOOL

Since the wise men have not spoken, I speak that
    am only a fool;
A fool that hath loved his folly,
Yea, more than the wise men their books or their
    counting houses, or their quiet homes,
Or their fame in men's mouths;
A fool that in all his days hath done never a prudent
    thing
Never hath counted the cost, nor recked if another
    reaped
The fruit of his mighty sowing, content to scatter
    the seed;
A fool that is unrepentant, and that soon at the end
    of all
Shall laugh in his lonely heart as the ripe ears fall
    to the reaping-hooks
And the poor are filled that were empty,
Tho' he go hungry.

I have squandered the splendid years that the Lord
    God gave to my youth
In attempting impossible things, deeming them
    alone worth the toil.
Was it folly or grace? Not men shall judge me, but
    God.

I have squandered the splendid years:
Lord, if I had the years I would squander them over
    again?
Aye, fling them from me!
For this I have heard in my heart, that a man shall
    scatter, not hoard,
Shall do the deed of to-day, nor take thought of
    to-morrow's teen,
Shall not bargain or huxter with God; or was it a
    jest of Christ's

And is this my sin before men, to have taken Him
    at His word?

The lawyers have sat in council, the men with the
    keen, long faces,
And said, "This man is a fool," and others have said,
    "He blasphemeth";
And the wise have pitied the fool that hath striven
    to give a life
In the world of time and space among the bulks of
    actual things,
To a dream that was dreamed in the heart, and that
    only the heart could hold.

O wise men, riddle me this: what if the dream come
    true?
What if the dream come true? and if millions
    unborn shall dwell
In the house that I shaped in my heart, the noble
    house of my thought?
Lord, I have staked my soul, I have staked the lives
    of my kin
On the truth of Thy dreadful word. Do not
    remember my failures,
But remember this my faith.

And so I speak.
Yea, ere my hot youth pass, I speak to my people
    and say:
Ye shall be foolish as I; ye shall scatter, not save;
Ye shall venture your all, lest ye lose what is
    more than all;
Ye shall call for a miracle, taking Christ at His word.
And for this I will answer, O people, answer here
    and hereafter,
O people that I have loved shall we not answer
    together?

THE REBEL

I am come of the seed of the people, the people that
    sorrow,
That have no treasure but hope,
No riches laid up but a memory
Of an Ancicnt glory.
My mother bore me in bondage, in bondage my
    mother was born,
I am of the blood of serfs:
The children with whom I have played, the men and
    women with whom I have eaten,
Have had masters over them, have been under the
    lash of masters,
And, though gentle, have served churls;
The hands that have touched mine, the dear hands
    whose touch is familiar to me,
Have worn shameful manacles, have been bitten at
    the wrist by manacles,
Have grown hard with the manacles and the
    task-work of strangers,
I am flesh of the flesh of these lowly, I am bone of
    their bone,
I that have never submitted;
I that have a soul greater than the souls of my
    people's masters,
I that have vision and prophecy and the gift of fiery
    speech,
I that have spoken with God on the top of His holy
    hill.

And because I am of the people, I understand the
    people,
I am sorrowful with their sorrow, I am
    hungry with their desire:
My heart has been heavy with the grief of mothers,
My eyes have been wet with the tears of children.
I have yearned with old wistful men,

And laughed or cursed with young men;
Their shame is my shame, and I have reddened for
    it,
Reddened for that they have served, they who
    should be free,
Reddened for that they have gone in want, while
    others have been full
Reddened for that they have walked in fear of
    lawyers and of their jailers
With their writs of summons and their handcuffs,
Men mean and cruel!
I could have borne stripes on my body rather than
    this shame of my people.

And now I speak, being full of vision;
I speak to my people, and I speak in my people's
    name to the masters of my people.
I say to my people that they are holy, that they are
    august, despite their chains,
That they are greater than those that hold them,
    and stronger and purer,
That they have but need of courage, and to call on
    the name of their God,
God the unforgetting, the dear God that loves the
    peoples
For whom He died naked, suffering shame.
And I say to my people's masters: Beware,
Beware of the thing that is coming, beware of the
    risen people,
Who shall take what ye would not give. Did ye think
    to conquer the people,
Or that Law is stronger than life and than men's
    desire to be free?
We will try it out with you, ye that have harried and
    held,
Ye that have bullied and bribed, tyrants, hypocrites,
    liars !

A SONG FOR MARY MAGDALENE

O woman of the gleaming hair,
(Wild hair that won men's gaze to thee)
Weary thou turnest from the common stare,
For the *shuiler* Christ is calling thee.

O woman of the snowy side,
Many a lover hath lain with thee,
Yet left thee sad at the morning tide,
But thy love Christ shall comfort thee.

O woman with the wild thing's heart,
Old sin hath set a snare for thee:
In the forest ways forspent thou art
But the hunter Christ shall pity thee.

THE RANN OF THE LITTLE PLAYMATE

Young Íosa plays with me every day,
(*With an óró and an iaró*)
Tig and Pookeen and Hide-in-the-Hay,
(*With an óró and an iaró*)
We race in the rivers with otters grey,
We climb the tall trees where red squirrels
    play,
We watch the wee lady-bird fly far away.
(*With an óró and an iaró and an úmbó éró!*)

CHRISTMAS 1915

O King that was born
To set bondsmen free,
In the coming battle,
Help the Gael!

THE MOTHER

I do not grudge them: Lord, I do not grudge
My two strong sons that I have seen go out
To break their strength and die, they and a few,
In bloody protest for a glorious thing,
They shall be spoken of among their people,
The generations shall remember them,
And call them blessed;
But I will speak their names to my own heart
In the long nights;
The little names that were familiar once
Round my dead hearth.
Lord, thou art hard on mothers:
We suffer in their coming and their going;
And tho' I grudge them not, I weary, weary
Of the long sorrow—And yet I have my joy:
My sons were faithful, and they fought.

THE WAYFARER

The beauty of the world hath made me sad,
This beauty that will pass;
Sometimes my heart hath shaken with great joy
To see a leaping squirrel in a tree,
Or a red lady-bird upon a stalk,
Or little rabbits in a field at evening,
Lit by a slanting sun,
Or some green hill where shadows drifted by
Some quiet hill where mountainy man hath sown
And soon would reap; near to the gate of Heaven;
Or children with bare feet upon the sands
Of some ebbed sea, or playing on the streets
Of little towns in Connacht,
Things young and happy.
And then my heart hath told me:
These will pass,
Will pass and change, will die and be no more,
Things bright and green, things young and happy;
And I have gone upon my way
Sorrowful.

Dual Language

AR THRÁ BHINN ÉADAIR

Ar thrá Bhinn Éadair
Briseann tonn le fuaim;
Screadann faoileán aonrach
Os cionn an chuain.

Ó lár an léana
Le hais Ghlas Naíon
Labhrann an traona
Ar feadh na hoích'.

Tá ceiliúr éanlaithe
I nGleann na Smól,
An lon 's an chéirseach
Ag cantain ceoil.

Tá soilse gréine
Ar thaobh Sléibh' Rua,
Is an ghaoth ag séideadh
Óna bharr anuas.

Ar chuan Dhún Laoghaire
Tá bád is long
Fá sheoltaibh gléasta
Ag treabhadh na dtonn.

Anseo in Éirinn
Dom féin, a bhráthair,
Is tusa i gcéin uaim
I bPáras áigh:

Mise ag féachaint
Ar chnoc is chuan,
Ar thrá Bhinn Éadair,
Is ar thaobh Sléibh' Rua;

ON THE STRAND OF HOWTH

On the strand of Howth
Breaks a sounding wave;
A lone sea-gull screams
Above the bay.

In the middle of the meadow
Beside Glasnevin
The corncrake speaks
All night long.

There is minstrelsy of birds
In Glenasmole,
The blackbird and thrush
Chanting music.

There is shining of sun
On the side of Slieverua,
And the wind blowing
Down over its brow.

On the harbour of Dunleary
Are boat and ship
With sails set
Ploughing the waves.

Here in Ireland,
Am I, my brother,
And you far from me
In gallant Paris,

I beholding
Hill and harbour,
The strand of Howth
And Slieverua's side,

Is tusa go réimeach
I bPáras mór
Na ríbhrugh n-aolda
Is na dtreathanslógh.

'S éard atáim a éileamh
Ort féin, a ghrá,
I bhfad i gcéin duit
Go smaoinír tráth

Ar phort an traona
Le hais Ghlas Naíon,
Ó lár an léana
Ag labhairt san oích';

Ar ghlór na héanlaithe
I nGleann na Smól,
Go sásta séiseach
Ag cantain ceoil;

Ar thrá Bhinn Éadair
Mar a mbriseann tonn,
'S ar chuan Dhún Laoghaire
Mar a luascann long;

Ar an ngréin ag scéitheadh
Ar thaobh Sléibh' Rua,
Is ar an ngaoth a shéideas
Óna bharr anuas!

And you victorious
In mighty Paris
Of the limewhite palaces
And the surging hosts;

And what I ask
Of you, beloved,
Far away
Is to think at times

Of the corncrake's tune
Beside Glasnevin
In the middle of the meadow,
Speaking in the night;

Of the voice of the birds
In Glenasmole
Happily, with melody,
Chanting music;

Of the strand of Howth
Where a wave breaks,
And the harbour of Dunleary,
Where a ship rocks;

On the sun that shines
On the side of Slieverua,
And the wind that blows
Down over its brow.

A ÉIN BHIG

(Gealbhan do fuaras ar lic mo dhorais lá
geimhridh agus é marbh)
A éin bhig!
Fuar liom do luí ar an lig:
A éin nár smuain riamh olc,
Trua triall an bháis ort!

O LITTLE BIRD

*(A sparrow which I found on my doorstep on
a day of winter.)*

O little bird!
Cold to me thy lying on the flag:
Bird, that never had an evil thought,
Pitiful the coming of death to thee!

BEAN tSLÉIBHE AG CAOINEADH
A MIC

Brón ar an mbás, 's é dhubh mo chroíse:
D'fhuadaigh mo ghrá is d'fhág mé cloíte,
Gan caraid gan compánach fá dhíon mo thíse
Ach an léan seo im' lár, is mé ag caoineadh!

Ag gabháil an tsléibhe dom tráthnóna
Do labhair an éanlaith liom go brónach,
Do labhair an naosc binn 's an crotach glórach
Ag faisnéis dom gur éag mo stórach.

Do ghlaoigh mé ort is do ghlór ní chualas,
Do ghlaoigh mé arís is freagra ní bhfuaras,
Do phóg mé do bhéal, is a Dhia, nárbh fhuar é!
Och, is fuar í do leaba sa gcillín uaigneach.

'S a uaigh fhódghlas 'na bhfuil mo leanbh,
A uaigh chaol bheag, ós tú a leaba,
Mo bheannacht ort, is na mílte beannacht
Ar na fódaibh glasa atá os cionn mo pheata.

Brón ar an mbás, ní féidir a shéanadh,
Leagann sé úr is críon le chéile—
'S a mhaicín mhánla, is é mo chéasadh
Do cholainn chaomh bheith ag déanamh
    créafóig' !

A WOMAN OF THE MOUNTAIN
KEENS HER SON

Grief on the death, it has blackened my heart:
It has snatched my love and left me desolate,
Without friend or companion under the roof of my
     house,
But this sorrow in the midst of me, and I keening.

As I walked the mountain in the evening
The birds spoke to me sorrowfully,
The sweet snipe spoke and the voiceful curlew
Relating to me that my darling was dead.

I called to you and your voice I heard not,
I called again and I got no answer,
I kissed your mouth, and O God how cold it was!
Ah, cold is your bed in the lonely churchyard.

O green-sodden grave in which my child is,
Little narrow grave, since you are his bed,
My blessing on you, and thousands of blessings
On the green sods that are over my treasure.

Grief on the death, it cannot be denied,
It lays low, green and withered together,—
And O gentle little son, what tortures me is
That your fair body should be making clay!

A MHIC BHIG NA gCLEAS

A mhic bhig na gcleas,
Is maith is feas dom
Go ndearnais míghníomh:
Can go fíor do locht.

Maithim duit, a linbh
An bhéil deirg bhoig:
Ní daorfar liom neach
Ar pheaca nár thuig.

Do cheann maiseach tóg
Go bpógad do bhéal:
Más fearrde aon dínn sin,
Is fearrde mise é.

Tá cumhracht id' phóig
Nachar fríth fós liom
I bpógaibh na mban
Ná i mbalsam a gcorp.

A mhic na rosc nglas,
An lasair sin id' ghnúis
De m'uamhan bheadh bán
Dá léifeá mo rúin.

An té 'gá bhfuil mo rúin,
Ní fiú é teagmháil leat:
Nach trua an dáil sin,
A mhic bhig na gcleas?

LITTLE LAD OF THE TRICKS

Little lad of the tricks,
Full well I know
That you have been in mischief:
Confess your fault truly.

I forgive you, child
Of the soft red mouth:
I will not condemn anyone
For a sin not understood.

Raise your comely head
Till I kiss your mouth:
If either of us is the better of that
I am the better of it.

There is fragrance in your kiss
That I have not found yet
In the kisses of women
Or in the honey of their bodies.

Lad of the grey eyes,
That flush in thy cheek
Would be white with dread of me
Could you read my secrets.

He who has my secrets
Is not fit to touch you:
Is not that a pitiful thing,
Little lad of the tricks?

NÍOR CRUINNÍODH LIOMSA ÓR

Níor cruinníodh liomsa ór;
An clú do fríth liom, d' fheoigh,
Sa ngrá do fuaras brón
Mo shaoghal do sheirg:

De ionmhas ná de ghlóir
Ní fhágfad i mo dheoidh
(Liomsa, a Dhia, is leor)
Ach m'ainm i gcroí linbh.

I HAVE NOT GARNERED GOLD

I have not garnered gold;
The fame I found hath perished;
In love I got but grief
That withered my life.

Of riches or of store
I shall not leave behind me
(Yet I deem it, O God, sufficient)
But my name in the heart of a child.

FORNOCHT DO CHONAC THU

Fornocht do chonac thu,
A áille na háille,
Is dhallas mo shúil
Ar eagla go stánfainn.

Do chualas do cheol,
A bhinne na binne,
Is do dhúnas mo chluas
Ar eagla go gclisfinn.

Do bhlaiseas do bhéal,
A mhilse na milse,
Is chruas mo chroí
Ar eagla mo mhillte.

Do dhallas mo shúil,
Is mo chluas do dhúnas,
Do chruas mo chroí
Is mo mhian do mhúchas;

Do thugas mo chúl
Ar an aisling a chumas,
'S ar an ród seo romham
M'aghaidh do thugas.

Do thugas mo ghnúis
Ar an ród seo romham,
Ar an ngníomh do-chím,
'S ar an mbás do-gheobhad.

RENUNCIATION

Naked I saw thee,
O beauty of beauty,
And I blinded my eyes
For fear I should fail.

I heard thy music,
O melody of melody,
And I closed my ears
For fear I should falter.

I tasted thy mouth,
O sweetness of sweetness,
And I hardened my heart
For fear of my slaying.

I blinded my eyes,
And I closed my ears,
I hardened my heart
And I smothered my desire.

I turned my back
On the vision I had shaped,
And to this road before me
I turned my face.

I have turned my face
To this road before me,
To the deed that I see
And the death I shall die.

MISE ÉIRE

Mise Éire:
Sine mé ná an Chailleach Bhéarra.

Mór mo ghlóir:
Mé a rug Cú Chulainn cróga.

Mór mo náir:
Mo chlann féin a dhíol a máthair.

Mise Éire:
Uaigní mé ná an Chailleach Bhéarra.

I AM IRELAND

I am Ireland:
I am older than the Old Woman of Beare.

Great my glory:
I that bore Cuchulainn the valiant.

Great my shame:
My own children that sold their mother.

I am Ireland:
I am lonelier than the Old Woman of Beare.

CRÓNÁN MNÁ SLÉLBHE

A chinnín óir, a choinneal mo thíse,
Déanfair eolas dá siúlann an tír seo.

A bhéilín bhoig do dheol mo chíocha,
Phógfaidh Muire thu ar a slí di.

A ghrua bheag chruinn is séimhe ná síoda,
Leagfaidh Íosa a láimhín mín ort.

Póga Mhuire ar bhéilín mo naíse,
Láimhín Chríost ar leiceann mo laoigh bhig!

Bí ciúin, a theach, 's a luichíní liatha,
Comhnaighidh anocht in bhur gcuasaibh iata.

A leamhana ar an bhfuinneoig, fillidh bhur sciatha,
Coscaidh bhur gcrónán, a chuileoga ciara.

A fheadóg 's a chrotaigh, thar mo theach ná triallaidh,
Ná labhair, a chadhain, ag dul thar an sliabh seo.

A dhúile an tsléibhe dhúisíos go hiarmhoch,
Ná corraighidh anocht go ngealaí grian díbh!

LULLABY OF A WOMAN
OF THE MOUNTAIN

Little gold head, my house's candle,
You will guide all wayfarers that walk this
    mountain.

Little soft mouth that my breast has known,
Mary will kiss you as she passes.

Little round cheek, O smoother than satin,
Jesus will lay His hand on you.

Mary's kiss on my baby's mouth,
Christ's little hand on my darling's cheek!

House, be still, and ye little grey mice,
Lie close to-night in your hidden lairs.

Moths on the window, fold your wings,
Little black chafers, silence your humming.

Plover and curlew, fly not over my house,
Do not speak, wild barnacle, passing over this
    mountain.

Things of the mountain that wake in the
night-time, Do not stir to-night till the daylight
    whitens!

AN DORD FÉINNE

'S é do bheatha, a bhean ba léannmhar
Dob' é ár gcreach do bheith i ngéibheann,
Do dhúthaigh bhreá i seilbh méirleach,
 'S tú díolta leis na Gallaibh.

  Óró, 's é do bheatha abhaile,
  Óró, 's é do bheatha abhaile,
  Óró, 's é do bheatha abhaile,
  Anois ar theacht an tsamhraidh.

A bhuí le Dia na bhfeart go bhfeiceam,
Muna mbímid beo ina dhiaidh ach seachtain,
Gráinne Mhaol is míle gaiscíoch
 Ag fógairt fáin ar Ghallaibh.

  Óró, 's é do bheatha abhaile,
  Óró, 's é do bheatha abhaile,
  Óró, 's é do bheatha abhaile,
  Anois ar theacht an tsamhraidh.

Tá Gráinne Mhaol ag teacht thar sáile,
Is Fianna Fáil 'na mbuidhin gharda,
Gaeil féin 's ní Francaigh ná Spáinnigh,
 Is ruagairt ar na Gallaibh!

  Óró, 's é do bheatha abhaile,
  Óró, 's é do bheatha abhaile,
  Óró, 's é do bheatha abhaile,
  Anois ar theacht an tsamhraidh.

THE DORD FEINNE

'Se do bheatha, O woman that wast sorrowful,
What grieved us was thy being in chains,
Thy beautiful country in the possession of rogues,
    And thou sold to the Galls,

> *Óró, 's é do bheatha abhaile,*
> *Óró, 's é do bheatha abhaile,*
> *Óró, 's é do bheatha abhaile,*
> Now at summer's coming!

Thanks to the God of miracles that we see,
Altho' we live not a week thereafter,
Gráinne Mhaol and a thousand heroes
    Proclaiming the scattering of the Galls!

> Óró, 's é do bheatha abhaile,
> *Óró, 's é do bheatha abhaile,*
> *Óró, 's é do bheatha abhaile,*
> Now at summer's coming!

Gráinne Mhaol is coming from over the sea,
The Fenians of Fál as a guard about her,
Gaels they, and neither French nor Spaniard,
    And a rout upon the Galls!

> Óró, 's é do bheatha abhaile,
> *Óró, 's é do bheatha abhaile,*
> *Óró, 's é do bheatha abhaile,*
> Now at summer's coming!

CAD CHUIGE DÍBH
DOM' CHIAPADH?

Cad chuige díbh dom' chiapadh, a mhiana mo chroí?
Dom' chiapadh is dom' phianadh de ló is d'oích',
Dom' fhiach mar do fiachófaí fia bocht ar shliabh,
Fia bocht fadtuirseach 's an chonairt ina dhiaidh?

Níl suaimhneas dom' phianas in uaigneas na gcnoc,
Ach uallgháir na bhfiagaí go huafar le clos,
Uallgháir mo mhiansa dom' fhiach gan spás—
'S a chona craosfhiaclacha, is fada bhur rás!

Níl sásamh i ndán dom' mhianaibh lem' ré,
Óir ní sásamh an sásamh do mhianas inné,
'S is cíocraí an chonairt den tsásamh do fuair—
'S go síoraí ní chodlód go gcodlaíod san uaigh.

WHY DO YE TORTURE ME?

Why are ye torturing me, O desires of my heart?
Torturing me and paining me by day and by
    night?
Hunting me as a poor deer would be hunted on a
    hill,
A poor long-wearied deer with the hound-pack
    after him?

There's no ease to my paining in the loneliness of
    the hills,
But the cry of the hunters terrifically to be heard,
The cry of my desires haunting me without
    respite,—
O ravening hounds, long is your run!

No satisfying can come to my desires while I live,
For the satisfaction I desired yesterday is no
    satisfaction,
And the hound-pack is the greedier of the
    satisfaction it has got,—
And forever I shall not sleep till I sleep in the
    grave.

A CHINN ÁLAINN

A chinn álainn na mná a ghrádhas,
I lár na hoíche cuimhním ort:
Ach filleann léargas le gile gréine—
Mo léan an chnumh chaol dod' chnaí anocht!

A ghlóir ionmhain dob íseal aoibhinn,
An fíor go gcualas trém' shuanaibh thu?
Nó an fíor an t-eolas atá dom' bheoghoin?
Mo bhrón, sa tuamba níl fuaim ná guth!

O LOVELY HEAD

O lovely head of the woman that I loved,
In the middle of the night I remember thee:
But reality returns with the sun's whitening,
Alas, that the slender worm gnaws thee
   to-night.

Beloved voice, that wast low and beautiful,
Is it true that I heard thee in my slumbers!
Or is the knowledge true that tortures me?
My grief, the tomb hath no sound or voice?

FADA LIOM DO THEACHT

Fada liom do theacht,
A sheaneachlaigh Dé,
A chara na gcarad,
Dom' scaradh lem' phéin.

A shiolla ar an ngaoith,
A choiscéim nach trom,
A lámh sa doircheacht,
Bhur dteacht is fada liom.

LONG TO ME THY COMING

Long to me thy coming,
Old henchman of God,
O friend of all friends,
To free me from my pain.

O syllable on the wind,
O footfall not heavy,
O hand in the dark,
Your coming is long to me.

RANN DO RINNEAS

Rann a rinneas i mo chroí
Don ridire, don ardrí,
Rann a rinneas do mo ghrá,
Do rí na rí, don tseanbhás:

Gaile liom ná soilse lae
Doircheacht do thí gidh dubhchré;
Binne liom ná ceol na stoc
Ciúnas do thí is a shíorthost.

A RANN I MADE

A rann I made within my heart
To the rider, to the high king,
A rann I made to my love,
To the king of kings, ancient death.

Brighter to me than light of day
The dark of thy house, tho' black clay;
Sweeter to me than the music of trumpets
The quiet of thy house and its eternal silence.

DO LEANBH IONMHAIN

A bhéil gháirigh, is é a chrás mé
Go mbiadh tú ag caí;
A ghné álainn, is é mo chás-sa
Go liathfaidh do lí.

A chinn uasail, ataoi uaibhreach,
Ach cromfair le brón;
'S is ní thruamhar bhím do tuar duit,
Nuair bhronnaim ort póg.

TO A BELOVED CHILD

Laughing mouth, what tortures me is
That thou shalt be weeping;
Lovely face, it is my pity
That thy brightness shall grow grey.

Noble head, thou art proud,
But thou shalt bow with sorrow;
And it is a pitiful thing I forbode for thee
Whenever I kiss thee.

TEACHT CHRÍOST

Do ghlanas mo chroí anocht
Amhail mhnaoi do ghlanfadh a teach
Roimh theacht dá leannán dá fios:
A leannáin, ná téirigh thart!

Do leathas doras mo chroí
Amhail fhear do-ghéanadh fleadh
Ar theacht i gcéin dá mhac:
A Mhic, is álainn do theacht!

CHRIST'S COMING

I have made my heart clean to-night
As a woman might clean her house
Ere her lover come to visit her:
O Lover, pass not by!

I have opened the door of my heart
Like a man that would make a feast
For his son's coming home from afar:
Lovely Thy coming, O Son!

Irish Poems

BETLEHEM

Síon is sneachta
Oighear ar aibhnibh,
Reoch anocht na réalta;
Cuing ar easaibh
Linnte ina leacaibh—
Brónach liom an saoghal!

Och! an mháthair
Mhodhúil mhánla,
Trua an seanóir críonna!
Bocht a n-áras,
A bhfoscadh i stábla,
Monuar! is dealbh an dídean!

Fuar an oíche!
Trua an Naoidhean!
Lom, mo chás, A leaba!
Tuargan gaoithe,
Cruatan geimhridh—
Olc do fháilte, a Leanbh!

Ceol sna Flaithis
Ag cór na n-aingeal,
Stoc is píob is cláirseach;
Glórtha neamhdha
Ag gabháil a gcaintic,
Is ag moladh Chríost, an tArd-Rí!

MÓRA DUIT, A THÍR ÁR nDÚCHAIS!

Móra duit, a thír ár ndúchais!
Dia dod' sheoladh slán!
Mochean dod' bheannaibh borba!
Mochean dod' leathanlochaibh!
Mochean dod' aibhnibh is dod' easaibh!
Dod' mhóintibh is dod' mhághaibh!
Is móra duit, a thír ár ndúchais!
Go mairirse go bráth!

Móra duit, a áitreabh éigse!
Dia dod' sheoladh slán!
Aoibhinn ceol do chláirseach,
Aoibhinn glór do shámhchrot,
Aoibhinn do scéalta is do dhréachta
Á síorghabháil ag baird!
Is móra duit, a áitreabh éigse!
Go mairirse go bráth!

Móra duit, a bhuime laochraí!
Dia dod' sheoladh slán!
Ag cosaint chlú is oinigh,
Ag cosaint chrú do chlainne,
Ag cosaint Chirt ar éigean Nirt,
Níor stríocais fós do námhaid!
Is móra duit, a bhuime laochraí!
Go mairirse go bráth!

Móra duit, a thír ár ndúchais!
Dia dod' sheoladh slán!
An fhaid 's is buan do bheanna,
An fhaid 's a ghluaiseas d'aibhne,
An fhaid is a mhairfeas féar is fearann,
Ní stadfam ó do ghrá!
Is móra duit, a thir ár ndúchais!
Dia dod' sheoladh slán!

A GHAELA NA PÁIRTE

A Ghaela na páirte
Ar greann libh Éire ársa,
A cnoca is a bánta,
A sléibhte maola arda,
A gleannta uaigneacha áille,
A leathanlocha breátha,
A haibhneacha ag snámhaíl
 Go mall ó thuaith go tuath;
A Ghaela is a mhuintir,
Ar geal libh clú bhur sinsear,
Na laochra is na ríthe
A d'fhág againn mar oidhreacht
A gcrógacht is a ndílseacht
Don mháthair ónar shíol
Siadsan is sinne, a dhaoine,
Is a bhfuil a gcuimhne buan;
A Ghaela is a chairde
Ar cuimhin libh teacht an Táilghinn,
Is na mílte naomh a d'áitigh
Ár dtír ó aimsir Phádraig,
Bríd, an mhaighdean mhánla,
Colm Cille 's ár bpátrún,
Éanna uasal Árann,
 'S na céadta nach luaim;
Tá scéal againn le léiriú
Ar naomh de naomhaibh Éireann,
Arbh iontach a thréithe,
Ar mhór le rá a léigheann,
A umhlaíocht is a fhéile,
A charthanacht is a dhaonnacht,
An sárfhear naofa Aongas,
 Do fuair ó Dhia gach bua.

Is tuigidhse, a chairde,
Gurbh iontach mar ghrádhaigh
An rífhear ar a dtráchtaim
Na páistí beaga bána;
Is gur chan sé ina dhántaibh
Gur gile leis an Ard-Rí
Anam glan an pháiste
Ná a bhfuil sna Flaithis thuas.

Is iarraimis ar Aongas
Ar Phádraig is ar Éanna,
Ar Cholm Cille is ar Bhríd ghil,
Beannacht ar an tigh seo.
Áiméan.

MACGHNÍOMHARTHA CHÚ CHULAINN

Incipit an Chaithréim

Scéal linn díbh, a uaisle Gaedheal,
A ghasra éachtach eolgach,
Scéal nachar fríth a shárú
In irsibh ársa Fódla.

Lá dár éirigh mac Neasa,
Rí neartmhar ógbhaidhe Uladh,
Do shuigh ar ard na hEamhna
I dteannta a laoch 's a churadh.

Ag imirt ann don mhacraidh,
Ar fhaiche an ríbhaile,
Do tháinig chucu an macaomh
Dob fhearr gaisce is gaile.

Do chuir trí chluiche orthu,
Ghabh á gcoscairt is á dtreascairt,
Gur nascadar air a gcomairc,
'S go mbíodh orthu ina cheannphort.

Fochtas an t-ardrí scéala
Den tréanmhac go mbuaghail:
' Is mé mac do dheirbhsheathar,
Seadanta mac Sualdaimh.'

Incipit an Dara Roinn

Scéal linn díbh, a uaisle Gaedheal,
A ghasra éachtach eolgach,
Scéal nachar fríth a shárú
In irsibh ársa Fódla.

Lá dá ndeachaigh mac Neasa,
Rí neartmhar ógbhaidhe Uladh,
D'ól fleidhe agus féasta
Ar éileamh an rícheird, Culann,

Fágadh i ndiaidh an ríthí
Mac míleata Sualdaimh,
Go ndeachaigh ar a lorgaibh
Go hoscartha buadhach.

Do bhí ag Culann rathmhar
Cú chalma chraosach chróga,
Thug fogha fán mac go feargach
Gur treascradh í sa gcomhrac.

Dúirt an t-óglach: ' A Chulainn,
Beadsa im' choin duit feasta.'
' Den ghníomh sin,' arsa Cafa,
' A mhacaoimh, Cú Chulainn t'ainmse. '

Incipit an Treas Roinn

Scéal linn díbh, a uaisle Gaedheal,
A ghasra éachtach eolgach,
Scéal nachar fríth a shárú
In irsibh ársa Fódla.

Lá dár éirigh mac Neasa,
Rí neartmhar ógbhaidhe Uladh,
Do tháinig chuige an macaomh,
Cú chalma chróga Chulainn.

D'iarr air airm agus trealamh,
D'fhág beannacht ag na hógaibh,
Is d'imigh roimhe ina charbad,
Do dhéanamh catha is comhraic.

Níor staon sé dá stárthaibh,
Go ráinig boird an chúige,
Gur mharaigh triúr mac Neachtain,
Cé fearúil na búraigh.

Scéal linn díbh, a uaisle Gaedheal,
A ghasra éachtach eolgach,
Scéal nachar fríth a shárú
In irisibh ársa Fódla.

MIONN

In ainm Dé,
Dar Críost a Aonmhac,
Dar Muire a Chaomh-mháthair,
Dar Pádraig Apstal Gael,
Dar dílseacht Choilm Chille,
Dar clú ár gcinidh,
Dar crú ár sinsear,
Dar dúnmharú Aodha Rua,
Dar bás truamhéalach Aodha Uí Néill,
Dar oidhe Eoghain Rua,
Dar mian an tSáirséalaigh le hucht a bháis,
Dar osna éagomhlainn an Ghearaltaigh,
Dar créachtaibh crólinnteacha Tone,
Dar fuil uasail Emmet,
Dar corpaibh an Ghorta,
Dar deoraibh deoraí nGael,
Do-bheirimid na mionna do-bheireadh ár sinsir
Go bhfuasclóimid do ghéibheann ár gcinidh,
Nó go dtitfimid bonn le bonn.
Áiméan.

Ó! 'BHEAN AN TÍ

Go Páras na Fraince a chuas dem' ruaig
(Beidh Boney in Éirinn le fáinne an lae,)
Gur chaitheas ann seachtain is ráithe
    ar cuaird.
(Is ó! 'bhean an tí, nach binn é mo scéal?)

Cia casfaí dom thall ach an faraire buan,
(Beidh Boney in Éirinn le fáinne an lae,)
Wolfe Tone do chlainn Shasan le fada
    thug fuath.
(Is ó! 'bhean an tí, nach binn é mo scéal?)

A lámh i mo láimhse go daingean do bhuail
(Beidh Boney in Éirinn le fáinne an lae,)
Is d'fhógair deargchogadh ar Ghallaibh
    an uabhair,
(Is ó! 'bhean an tí, nach binn é mo scéal?)

Tá loingeas na Fraince ar snámh ar an gcuan,
(Beidh Boney in Éirinn le fáinne an lae,)
Ar Éirinn a dtriall roimh mhaidin Dia Luain.
(Is ó! 'bhean an tí, nach binn é mo scéal?)

Seo éirleach is scaipeadh, fán fada is ruaig
(Beidh Boney in Éirinn le fáinne an lae,)
Ar Ghallaibh na cruinne, is olc linn an scuain.
(Is ó! 'bhean an tí, nach binn é mo scéal?)

Iar-Fhocal

le Michael Davitt

Agus mé i mbun pinn anseo ag baile, i ndeireadh Lúnasa 1993, tá ceol Bhono agus U2 le clos beo óna stáitse Zooropa míle slí uaim. Is dócha go bhfuil 40,000 éigin duine i láthair. Tá filíocht Phádraig Mhic Phiarais á léamh agam. Ba dheacair codarsnacht níos déine a shamhlú. Ach mar sin féin, nuair a bheidh an ceol thart, an chumhacht leictreonach sin ar fad curtha as, beidh cuid acusan ag filleadh abhaile ar dhomhan príobháid-each a tharlódh a bheith chomh dorcha céanna le domhan inmheánach na ndánta seo os mo chomhair. Inniu b'fhéidir go bhfuil tuiscintí beaga breise ann faoi thimpeallacht inmheánach an duine, na galair dhubh-acha, na hailsí spioradálta, an comhdhéanamh collaíoch agus tá téarnamh ann ar an taobh seo den bhás don té a shanntaíonn.

A raibh lasmuigh de chraiceann Phádraig: Éire dheireadh céid/thús céid, daoine, áiteanna, nithe, imeachtaí, cathanna, tránna, tinte cnámh, beola garsún, cíocha ban, An Bhreatain, b'in í a thimpeallacht shea-chtrach. Ach bhí timpeallacht eile istigh ann, laistigh dá chraiceann: braistintí, spreanganna, mianta, mothúcháin, smaointe, físeanna, borrthaí meabhrach agus cruthaith-eachta agus an phian sin ar fad, an féinamhras, an féintrua, an féinfhuath, an t-éagumas, an t-éadóchas—och, dob fhuar í a leaba ina chillín uaigneach.

Ach bhí droichead aige idir an dá thimpeallacht, an fhilíocht. "Trasnaigh, a léitheoir," adeir an file maith. "Sa

75

diabhal duit, fan amuigh," adeir an rannaire. Ardfhile ab ea an Piarsach. Chuaigh i bhfiontar. Lig isteach i nguairneán a chuid smaointe agus a mhothúchán sinn feasta is go brách i ndornán dánta snoite, ceolmhara, corraitheacha, ionraice, uaigneacha. Ar léamh na ndánta seo arís dom as an nua gan aird ar na miotais ná na frithmhiotais a leanann ainm an fhile féin, is ionadh liom gan puinn tráchta bheith riamh ar an bPiarsach mar fhíor-cheannródaí nuafhilíocht na Gaeilge.

"Ar Thrá Bhinn Éadair" an chéad dán Gaeilge a chuir sé i gcló riamh (sa *Chlaidheamh Soluis*, 1905, faoin ainm cleite Coimín Ó Cualáin).

> Ar Thrá Bhinn Éadair
> Briseann tonn le fuaim;
> Screadann faoileán aonrach
> Os cionn an chuain.

(Féach an feabhas a chuir sé ar líne 2 thuas i véarsa 12: "mar a mbriseann tonn"). Tá an droichead, dá ghuagaí, á thógáil cheana. Bhraithfeá láithreach gur ann féin atá scread an fhaoileáin aonraigh. Faoi thráth *Suantraidhe agus Goltraidhe, (1914),* bheadh an chonairt inmheánach scaoilte amach ar fud an bhaill.

> Níl sásamh i ndán dom' mhianaibh lem' ré,
> Óir ní sásamh an sásamh do mhianas inné,
> 'S is cíocraí an chonairt den tsásamh do fuair—
> 'S go síoraí ní chodlód go gcodlaíod san uaigh.
> ("Cad Chuige Díbh Dom' Chiapadh")

Níl aon oidhre air ach Seán Ó Ríordáin:

> Is atuirseach an intinn
> A thit in iomar doimhin na saoirse,
> Ní mhaireann cnoc dar chruthaigh Dia ann,
> Ach cnoic theibí, sainchnoic shamhlaíochta,

Is bíonn gach cnoc díobh lán de mhianta
Ag dreapadóireacht gan chomhlíonadh,
Níl teora leis an saoirse
Ná le cnoca na samhlaíochta,
Ná níl teora leis na mianta,
Ná faoiseamh
Le fáil.
(" Saoirse", *Eireaball Spideoige*, 1952)

Bhí gort na timpeallachta inmheánaí treafa ag Pádraig
Mac Pairais leathchéad bliain sarar scaoil an Ríordánach a
chonairt féin amach ar fud an bhaill. Deinim amach gur
dealraitheach go mór Seán le Pádraig mar fhile; an-cheard-
aithe teanga iad beirt agus tá an "brón do-inste" sin ina
ndánta araon.

Tá "A Mhic Bhig na gCleas" pléite go fuaimintiúil ag
Ciarán Ó Coigligh ina leabhar *Filíocht Ghaeilge
Phádraig Mhic Phiarais* (An Clóchomhar, 1981). Is léir
gur bhain an dán stangadh as a lán nuair a foilsíodh é
in *An Macaomh*, 1909. Níor chuir Pádraig Mac Piarais,
file agus príomhoide scoil bhuachaillí, fiacail ann:

Do cheann maiseach tóg
Go bpógad do bhéal:
Más fearrde aon dínn sin,
Is fearrde mise é.

Tá cumhracht id' phóig
Nachar fríth fós liom
I bpógaibh na mban
Ná i mbalsam a gcorp.

Dán dána péidifiliach, nó maoithneachas neamhurch-
óideach? Deir Ó Coigligh: ". . . is deacair a chreidiúint
gur chlaonta neamhchomhfhiosacha ar fad, na claonta
follasacha péidifiliacha a fhaightear ina chuid scríbh-
neoireachta. Cibé ar bith cé na claonta gnéasacha a bhí

77

ann, ní bhaineann siad blas ar bith dá cháil mar thírghráthóir ná mar fhear liteartha."

Is mór gan amhras idir fantaisíocht ghnéasach phéidifíliach agus mianta múchta péidifíliacha. Ar deireadh thiar níl sna póganna etc., nó a n-éagmais, ach comharthaí sóirt i dtimpeallacht Phádraig do chorraíl níos bunúsaí istigh ann féin. Tagann an chorraíl sin chun anfa sa dán "Fornocht do Chonac Thu", sméar mullaigh a shaothair fhileata. Níl aon áit is léire a nochtar dúinn an dalladh, an dúnadh, an chruachan, an cúlú ó aisling a bheithe féin. Féach milseacht shearbh na s-anna leathana:

> Do dhallas mo shúil
> Is mo chluas do dhúnas,
> Do chruas mo chroí
> Is mo mhian do mhúchas;

Féach seirfean milis na s-anna caola:

> Do bhlaiseas do bhéal,
> A mhilse na milse...

Duine atá ar snámh ar éigean sa duibheagán inmheánach atá anseo, greim an fhir bháite aige ar raic na filíochta. Tóir ar iomláine, ar fholláine, dó gníomh cruthaitheach na filíochta, iarracht ar an timpeallacht anfach istigh a cheansú. Ní foláir nó bhain Pádraig Mac Piarais an staid tharchéimniúil chruthaitheach amach agus é i mbun dánta mar "Fornocht..." agus "Bean tSléibhe..." agus fiú "Óró Sé do Bheatha Abhaile" agus ar feadh tamaillín bhí sé saor—focail, físeanna, mothúcháin agus intleacht ag rince gan scáth ná eagla agus sú álainn cruálach na filíochta ag stealladh tríd ar dalladh. Ach thiomáin na "cona craosfhiaclacha" i dtreo eile é ag lorg faoisimh.

Agus tú id sheasamh i gcoinne an fhalla, a Phádraig Mhic Phiarais, púicín ort, ag fanacht leis an bhfocal deireanach a chloisfeá, FIRE ! Arbh in é an faoiseamh a bhí uait?

An bhfuair tú é?

RENUNCIATION: P. H. PEARSE

Naked I saw thee, O beauty beyond beauty,
And I blinded my eyes for fear I would fail;
My palms were dry and my racked body shivering
When I screamed awake from her teasing laughter.

> No longer can I feel my face under this
>   hardening skin,
> they have run together under rain and dried in
>   the heat
> of platforms where my voice invented a nation
>   to live in
> among the haunted eyes staring from the faces
>   of defeat.

Christ I see Thee in Thy rituals and certainty,
Shield me in the confines of your lonely march,
My mind knows the fever of a barefoot boy's kiss,
Let the cool wafter of your body slacken my thrist.

> Armed men believe I command them, but they
>   lead me
> Out of myself into this role where I may
>   express,
> by a million doves of flame released over the
>   town,
> how when the heart cannot open it must burn
>   down.

Dermot Bolger